FIERCE PREDATORS

by **Anna Graham**
Consultant: Clint Twist

BEARPORT
PUBLISHING COMPANY, INC.
New York, New York

Picture credits (t=top; b=bottom; c=center; l=left; r=right) Corbis: 6-7 all, 9t, 10-11 all, 12-13 all, 14-15 all, 16-17 all, 20-21 all, 26t. FLPA: 8-9c, 18-19 all, 22-23 all, 24-25 all.

Every effort has been made to trace the copyright holders, and we apologize in advance for any unintentional omissions. We would be pleased to insert the appropriate acknowledgments in any subsequent edition of this publication.

Library of Congress Cataloging-in-Publication Data
Graham, Anna.
  Fierce predators / by Anna Graham.
    p. cm. — (Top 10s)
  Includes index.
  ISBN 1-59716-068-7 (lib. bdg.) — ISBN 1-59716-105-5 (pbk.)
1. Predatory animals—Juvenile literature. I. Title. II. Series.

QL758.G72 2006
591.5'3—dc22
                              2005010286

Copyright © 2006 Bearport Publishing Company, Inc. All rights reserved. No part of this publication may be reproduced in whole or in part, stored in a retrieval system, or transmitted in any form or by any means, electronic, mechanical, photocopying, recording, or otherwise, without written permission from the publisher.

For more information, write to Bearport Publishing Company, Inc., 101 Fifth Avenue, Suite 6R, New York, New York 10003. Printed in the United States of America.

1 2 3 4 5 6 7 8 9 10

Introduction 4
Leopard (No. 10) 6
Coyote (No. 9) 8
Polar Bear (No. 8) 10
Royal Bengal Tiger (No. 7) 12
Cheetah (No. 6) 14
Great Horned Owl (No. 5) 16
Nile Crocodile (No. 4) 18
African Lion (No. 3) 20
Orca (Killer Whale) (No. 2) 22
Great White Shark (No. 1) 24
Close But Not Close Enough 26
Stats 28
Glossary 30
Index 32

INTRODUCTION

This book presents the world's Top 10 **predators**. Predators are natural-born killers. They must kill in order to eat. Many different animals are predators. Which one is the best? Our Top 10 predators were rated on a scale of one to ten in the following categories:

Size and weight are important for a predator. Being large and heavy makes it easier to overpower and kill **prey**. Large predators are also able to attack bigger animals. We gave our predators a combined score based on their size and weight. We also considered the average size of the prey for each animal.

It's much easier to catch prey when you are fast. In addition to a predator's speed, we looked at whether the animal could leap, and how far. We gave extra points to crocodiles because they can move on land and in water.

NO. 7 | ROYAL BENGAL TIGER

One of the largest kinds of tigers, this fierce predator is often called the "biggest of the big cats." The Royal Bengal tiger is found in parts of northern India and Pakistan. Like all tigers, it is a deadly hunter, and it can develop a taste for human flesh.

BODY MASS
The Bengal tiger weighs between 441–551 pounds (200–250 kg). It can measure 9 feet (3 m) in length.

TEETH AND CLAWS
The Bengal tiger has strong, sharp claws and powerful jaws filled with 30 sharp teeth.

SPEED
A tiger can only run short distances. However, it can reach a speed of nearly 37 miles per hour (60 kph).

No two tigers have exactly the same pattern of stripes.

4

TEETH AND CLAWS

4/10

This category looks at the deadly weapons predators use to kill their prey. We based our score on the number, length, and sharpness of a predator's teeth and claws.

PREY

3/10

Most predators will attack anything that they can kill and eat. For this category, points were given based on the size and variety of the prey that is normally eaten. Predators that sometimes feast on human flesh were awarded extra points.

This big cat leaps onto its prey with outstretched claws.

PREY

The Bengal tiger will attack animals larger than itself. Its main prey is deer. It can eat more than 88 pounds (40 kg) of meat at one time.

KILLER INSTINCT

When the Bengal tiger leaps onto its prey, it digs in with its claws. Then it uses its weight to drag the victim to the ground.

EXTREME SCORES

The Bengal tiger is a large, powerful predator with a strong body, sharp teeth, and deadly claws.

BODY MASS **6/10**

SPEED **7/10**

TEETH AND CLAWS **4/10**

KILLER INSTINCT **5/10**

PREY **3/10**

= TOTAL SCORE **25/50**

13

KILLER INSTINCT

5/10

Here we looked at the style of each predator's attack. We gave points for hunting technique and **camouflage**. Additional points were given to predators that were able to surprise their victims, or had highly developed senses for locating prey.

5

NO.10 | LEOPARD

The leopard is a deadly predator that only comes out to hunt at night. Powerful muscles make it the strongest climber of the big cats, which also include lions, tigers, cheetahs, and jaguars. The leopard lives in warm and cool **climates** throughout Asia and Africa. It is found in plains, deserts, and rain forests.

BODY MASS
This skillful hunter weighs about 143 pounds (65 kg). Most leopards have **pale** fur with black spots. Some, however, are entirely black. These black leopards are known as panthers.

SPEED
When running at top speed, a leopard can reach about 37 miles per hour (60 kph). It can leap across a gap 20 feet (6 m) wide.

KILLER INSTINCT
This big cat may sneak up on its prey through tall grass. Sometimes it waits on a tree branch. It then jumps down to sink its teeth into its victim's neck.

Spotted fur provides excellent camouflage when hunting prey.

TEETH AND CLAWS
Leopards have curved claws that end in very sharp points.

PREY
The leopard can attack and kill prey as big as a giraffe. However, it mainly hunts smaller **mammals** such as deer and wild pigs.

Many predators, such as leopards, have eyes at the front of their heads.

EXTREME SCORES

This nighttime predator is a deadly hunter with powerful muscles and sharp claws.

BODY MASS 4/10

SPEED 6/10

TEETH AND CLAWS 3/10

KILLER INSTINCT 3/10

PREY 5/10

= **TOTAL SCORE**

21/50

7

NO.9 | COYOTE

The coyote is a North American wild dog that has **adapted** to many kinds of **environments**. It is found from the hot deserts of Mexico to the frozen forests of Alaska and Canada. The coyote is a highly **efficient** predator that hunts by both night and day.

BODY MASS
The coyote is a medium-sized animal. Its body is about 3 feet (1 m) long. It weighs about 44 pounds (20 kg).

SPEED
A coyote has a top speed of about 31 miles per hour (50 kph). It can jump over a fence that is 8 feet (2 m) tall.

A coyote uses its eyes, ears, and nose to find its prey.

TEETH AND CLAWS
Its claws are sharp, but teeth are the coyote's main weapons. It has 42 teeth in all.

Parents fetch food for young coyote pups.

KILLER INSTINCT

The coyote usually hunts alone. It can chase prey over long distances without getting tired. It has an excellent sense of smell for sniffing out prey hiding underground.

PREY

The coyote hunts a wide variety of prey. It kills mainly small mammals, such as mice, rabbits, and squirrels. However, it also catches birds, snakes, and lizards.

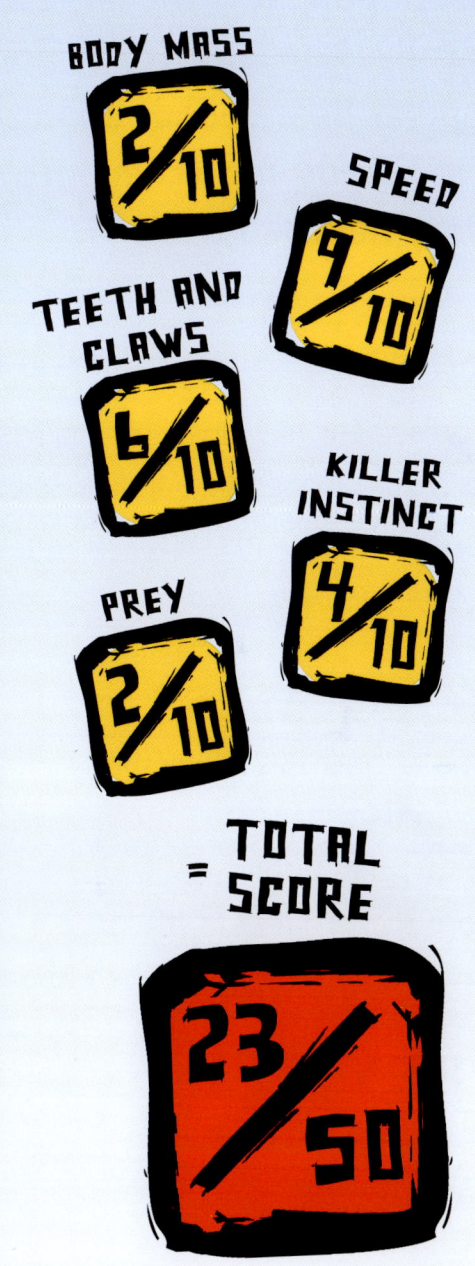

EXTREME SCORES

Whether living in grasslands or deserts, this speedy predator has no trouble catching its prey.

BODY MASS 2/10
SPEED 9/10
TEETH AND CLAWS 6/10
KILLER INSTINCT 4/10
PREY 2/10

= TOTAL SCORE 23/50

9

NO.8 | POLAR BEAR

The polar bear lives in the **arctic** region surrounding the North Pole. It is the largest and most powerful predator that lives on land. It has nothing to fear—except hunger. A polar bear spends about half its waking life hunting. It succeeds in catching prey only one or two times for every hundred tries.

TEETH AND CLAWS
A polar bear has long, sharp claws that can easily rip through skin and muscle. Its powerful jaws can crunch through bones.

BODY MASS
A polar bear has a huge body covered in shaggy fur. It can weigh up to 1,543 pounds (700 kg). It is more than 10 feet (3 m) long.

PREY
Polar bears mainly hunt seals. However, they also catch fish, seabirds, walruses, and reindeer.

White fur provides camouflage against the snowy landscape.

KILLER INSTINCT

The polar bear usually catches seals that are on land or have come to the water's surface to breathe. Sometimes a polar bear will break through ice to get at a seal.

SPEED

A polar bear can run across snow and ice at speeds of up to 25 miles per hour (40 kph). These animals are also excellent swimmers.

Powerful muscles are the key to the polar bear's deadly attack.

EXTREME SCORES

Protected from the cold by a thick fur coat, this arctic killer is a powerful predator.

BODY MASS
8/10

SPEED
5/10

TEETH AND CLAWS
4/10

KILLER INSTINCT
2/10

PREY
5/10

= TOTAL SCORE
24/50

11

NO.7 | ROYAL BENGAL TIGER

One of the largest kinds of tigers, this fierce predator is often called the "biggest of the big cats." The Royal Bengal tiger is found in parts of northern India and Pakistan. Like all tigers, it is a deadly hunter, and it can develop a taste for human flesh.

BODY MASS
The Bengal tiger weighs between 441–551 pounds (200–250 kg). It can measure 9 feet (3 m) in length.

No two tigers have exactly the same pattern of stripes.

TEETH AND CLAWS
The Bengal tiger has strong, sharp claws and powerful jaws filled with 30 sharp teeth.

SPEED
A tiger can only run short distances. However, it can reach a speed of nearly 37 miles per hour (60 kph).

This big cat leaps onto its prey with outstretched claws.

PREY
The Bengal tiger will attack animals larger than itself. Its main prey is deer. It can eat more than 88 pounds (40 kg) of meat at one time.

KILLER INSTINCT
When the Bengal tiger leaps onto its prey, it digs in with its claws. Then it uses its weight to drag the victim to the ground.

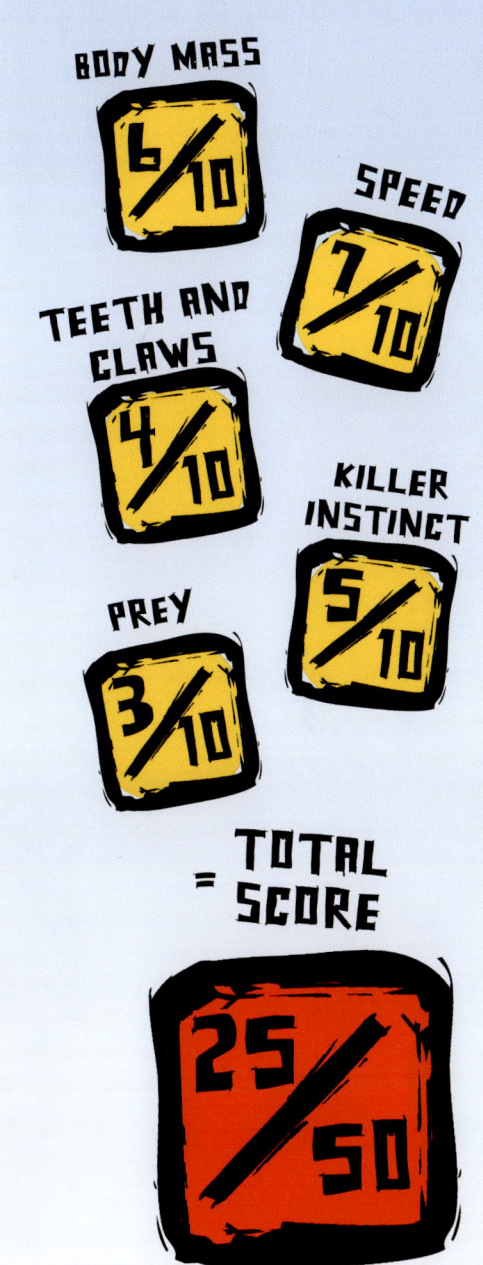

EXTREME SCORES

The Bengal tiger is a large, powerful predator with a strong body, sharp teeth, and deadly claws.

BODY MASS
6/10

SPEED
7/10

TEETH AND CLAWS
4/10

KILLER INSTINCT
5/10

PREY
3/10

= TOTAL SCORE
25/50

13

NO. 6 | CHEETAH

The cheetah can run faster than any other animal on Earth. It is one of the smallest of the big cats. However, it is also one of the deadliest. The cheetah lives on the grasslands of Africa, where it uses its speed to catch fast-running prey.

BODY MASS
The cheetah has a slim, light body. It weighs only about 88–99 pounds (40–45 kg).

The cheetah's sharp eyesight helps it find prey.

SPEED
Over short distances, a cheetah can reach a speed of more than 68 miles per hour (109 kph).

TEETH AND CLAWS
The cheetah attacks with both teeth and claws. The claws help a cheetah hook prey during a chase.

14

Sharp claws and teeth drag down a helpless victim.

KILLER INSTINCT

A cheetah usually hunts during the day. It silently creeps through the grass. When it is close enough to its prey, it launches a high-speed attack.

PREY

The cheetah hunts rabbits and small mammals. It also goes after larger prey such as zebras and antelopes.

EXTREME SCORES

No animal can run fast enough to escape the high-speed attack of this predator.

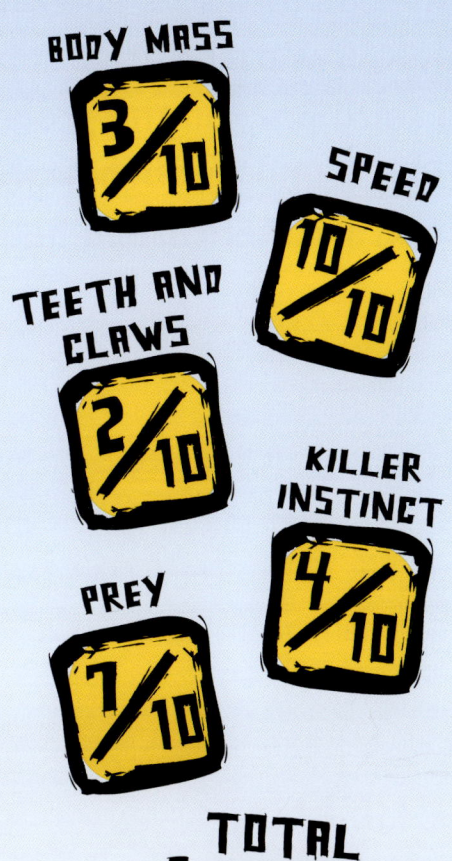

BODY MASS
3/10

SPEED
10/10

TEETH AND CLAWS
2/10

KILLER INSTINCT
4/10

PREY
7/10

= TOTAL SCORE
26/50

15

NO. 5 | GREAT HORNED OWL

The great horned owl can kill prey up to three times its own size. This bird attacks silently and without warning. It swoops down from its **perch** to seize prey on the ground. The great horned owl is found throughout North America, Central America, and South America.

BODY MASS
The great horned owl weighs about 6 pounds (3 kg). The female owls are larger than the males.

SPEED
This owl can reach a top flying speed of about 37 miles per hour (60 kph).

TEETH AND CLAWS
The great horned owl has no teeth. However, it does have a sharp **beak** for tearing flesh. Its main weapons are the sharp pointed **talons** on its feet.

Sharp eyes and good hearing are the key to the owl's success as a hunter.

KILLER INSTINCT

The great horned owl is most active at night. It uses its sense of sight and hearing to find prey. The owl dives down from high perches to snatch its victims.

PREY

Great horned owls are able to kill animals as big as skunks, foxes, and even porcupines.

The color of the owl's feathers provides excellent camouflage against tree trunks and branches.

EXTREME SCORES

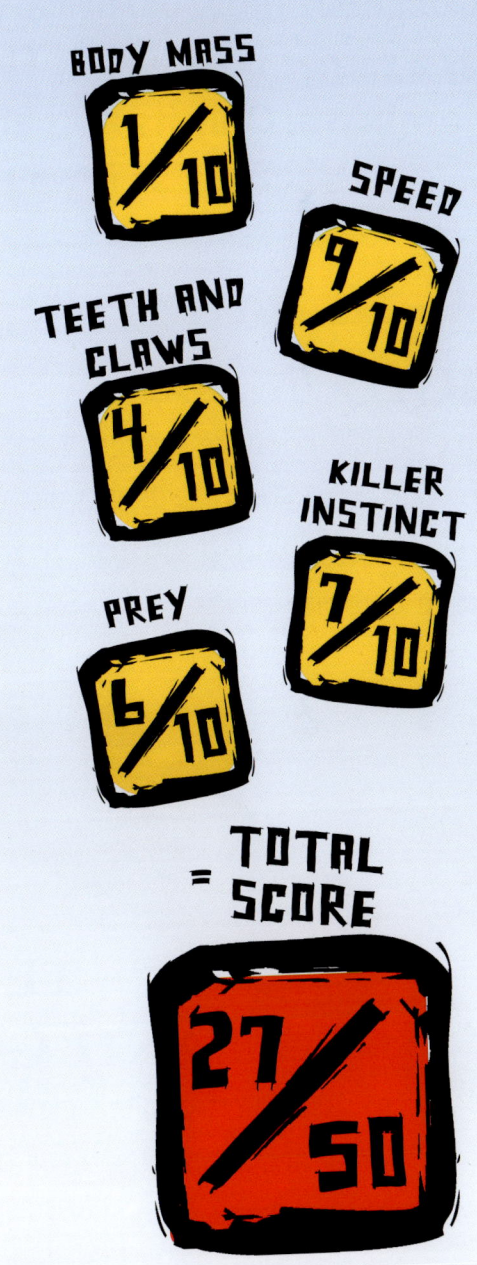

This bird is a silent killer that swoops down out of the darkness without warning.

BODY MASS 1/10
SPEED 9/10
TEETH AND CLAWS 4/10
KILLER INSTINCT 7/10
PREY 6/10

= TOTAL SCORE 27/50

17

NO.4 | NILE CROCODILE

The Nile crocodile is found in rivers, lakes, and swamps throughout most of Africa. It is a fierce killer. However, it is a rather lazy hunter. This large **reptile** prefers to lie in **ambush**. Only its eyes and **nostrils** can be seen above the river's surface as it waits for its prey.

BODY MASS

This deadly creature can grow up to 20 feet (6 m) in length. It is covered in natural **armor** made of bony scales.

A crocodile swims by using its flattened tail as a paddle.

TEETH AND CLAWS

The crocodile's claws are fairly dull. They are mainly used for digging nests in the riverbank. Long jaws full of sharp teeth are the Nile crocodile's main weapons.

SPEED

The Nile crocodile swims at about 4–6 miles per hour (6–10 kph). On land it can run at almost twice that speed.

These long, sharp teeth can cause terrible wounds.

KILLER INSTINCT

Like other reptiles, the Nile crocodile can bite, but it cannot chew. Small prey is swallowed whole. Larger prey is dragged under water to drown.

PREY

Small prey include fish and waterbirds. However, animals as big as buffalo and giraffes are attacked when they drink or cross rivers.

EXTREME SCORES

At first glance, it might look like a log floating in the water. However, that "log" is actually one of the most feared of all predators.

BODY MASS 7/10
SPEED 3/10
TEETH AND CLAWS 8/10
KILLER INSTINCT 8/10
PREY 6/10

= TOTAL SCORE 32/50

19

NO. 3 | AFRICAN LION

Although it is famous as the "king of the jungle," the African lion is rarely seen in a jungle. This powerful predator prefers open grasslands. Most big cats hunt alone. However, the African lion often hunts in small groups of three to eight animals.

BODY MASS
The male African lion is larger than the female. It weighs up to 551 pounds (250 kg).

SPEED
The African lion is not a fast runner. It can, however, reach about 34 miles per hour (55 kph) over very short distances.

TEETH AND CLAWS
Five claws on each paw, and powerful jaws with 30 sharp teeth make this a deadly beast.

The lion is Africa's top predator.

20

Male lions are the only big cats with a mane of long fur.

KILLER INSTINCT

Lions usually **cooperate** with one another when hunting. Several members of a lion group will try to drive the prey toward other lions.

PREY

The African lion hunts mainly large mammals such as zebras, impalas, and wildebeests.

EXTREME SCORES

Hunting in groups gives this big cat a deadly advantage over all the others.

BODY MASS
6/10

SPEED
8/10

TEETH AND CLAWS
5/10

KILLER INSTINCT
7/10

PREY
8/10

= TOTAL SCORE
34/50

21

NO. 2 ORCA (KILLER WHALE)

The orca is a toothed whale that is closely related to dolphins and porpoises. This **marine** mammal is found in seas and oceans around the world. It prefers cool water and is rarely seen in the **tropics**. The orca deserves its popular name—the killer whale—because it is a deadly predator with no natural enemies.

BODY MASS
An adult orca measures more than 27 feet (8 m) in length. It can weigh up to 22,046 pounds (10,000 kg).

SPEED
Orcas are fast swimmers and can reach speeds of 31 miles per hour (50 kph) for short distances when chasing prey.

TEETH AND CLAWS
An orca has 40–46 large, pointed teeth. However, it cannot chew and has to swallow its prey whole.

KILLER INSTINCT
Orcas often live and hunt in small family groups that are known as pods. The members of a pod may hunt together. However, an orca will also hunt sea lions on its own.

The orca has a distinctive black-and-white color.

The smiling face of a born killer

PREY
The orca feeds mainly on fish, especially salmon and squid. It also hunts dolphins, whales, seals, sea lions, penguins, and marine turtles.

EXTREME SCORES

This mammal is one of the biggest predators on Earth—about 10 tons (9 metric tons) of killing power.

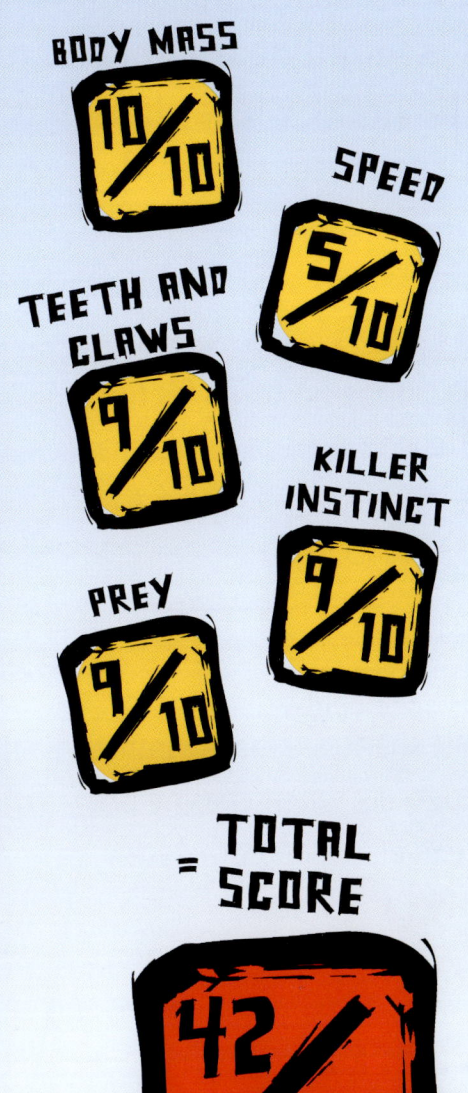

BODY MASS — 10/10
SPEED — 5/10
TEETH AND CLAWS — 9/10
KILLER INSTINCT — 9/10
PREY — 9/10

= TOTAL SCORE

42/50

23

NO. 1 | GREAT WHITE SHARK

With jaws more than 2 feet (61 cm) wide, the great white shark is the world's deadliest and most dangerous predator. It is found near cool and mild coastlines across the globe. The great white shark has a very strong sense of smell. It can detect wounded prey several miles (km) away.

BODY MASS
Measuring up to 26 feet (8 m) in length, a great white shark can weigh more than 6,614 pounds (3,000 kg).

SPEED
This shark is a fast swimmer, especially when chasing prey. It can also leap completely out of the water.

TEETH AND CLAWS
Rows of triangular teeth line the great white's massive jaws. Each tooth is razor sharp.

KILLER INSTINCT
The great white attacks with a rapid, twisting **lunge** that tears a huge chunk of flesh from the victim. The shark then waits for the victim to die from loss of blood.

These teeth are designed to slice rather than grip.

Each tooth lasts for less than a year before it is replaced by a new one.

PREY

The great white shark mainly hunts seals, dolphins, and large fish (including other sharks). However, the great white will attack anything it thinks it can eat.

EXTREME SCORES

Our top predator is the most efficient and ferocious hunter on Earth.

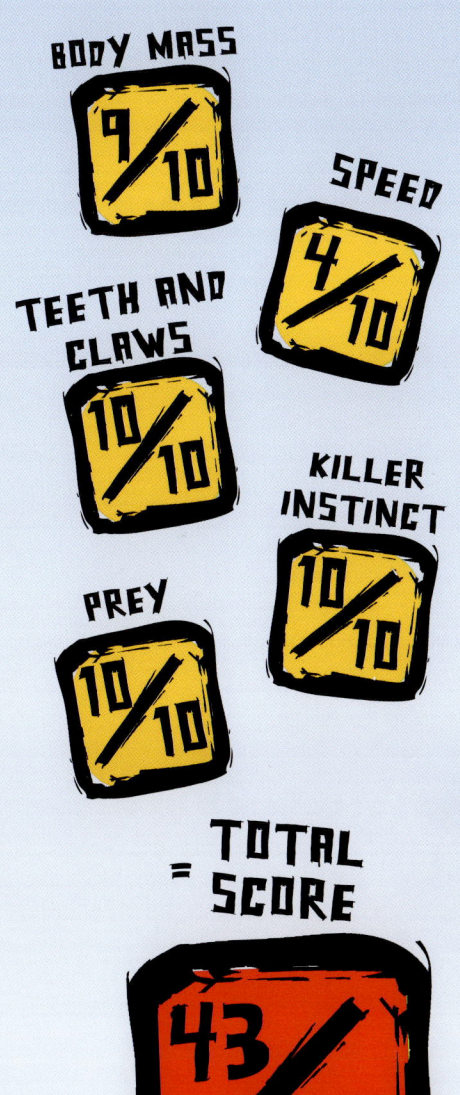

BODY MASS 9/10

SPEED 4/10

TEETH AND CLAWS 10/10

KILLER INSTINCT 10/10

PREY 10/10

= TOTAL SCORE 43/50

25

CLOSE
BUT NOT CLOSE ENOUGH

Before deciding our Top 10 predators, we also considered these animals. All of them are skillful hunters, but they are not quite good enough to make the Top 10.

BALD EAGLE

The bald eagle is the national bird of the United States. It is not really bald, however. It has white feathers on its head and neck that make it look bald from a distance. It is a large, powerful bird that weighs up to 13 pounds (6 kg). It has a wingspan of up to 8 feet (2 m). The bald eagle is especially fond of fish. It will swoop down to grab salmon in its sharp talons.

TARANTULA

Tarantulas are the largest of all spiders. They are found throughout tropical regions. The biggest tarantulas have a leg span of nearly 12 inches (30 cm). They can move very quickly. Tarantulas do not spin webs. They are hunters that prowl around at night looking for prey such as mice and small birds.

VAMPIRE BAT
This small South American mammal is known for its diet. It feeds on the blood of other mammals. The vampire bat does not actually suck blood. Instead, it bites its victim to make the blood flow and then laps it up with its tongue. Although it can fly, this bat likes to walk. It is actually more likely to attack its prey from the ground.

WOLVERINE
The wolverine is the largest and fiercest member of the weasel family. It lives in the forests of Europe, Asia, and North America. The wolverine measures up to 5 feet (2 m). It weighs about 33 pounds (15 kg). It chases after small prey such as rabbits. It will also climb trees so that it can jump down on large prey such as deer.

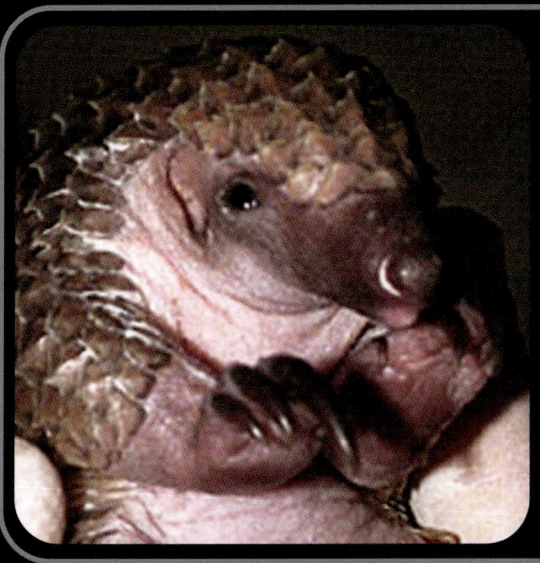

PANGOLIN
This strange scale-covered mammal is found in Africa and Asia. Although it is not fierce, the pangolin is a mighty hunter. It uses its powerful claws to burrow into termite mounds and ant nests. It then slurps up their tasty eggs with its long tongue. The unique coat of hard scales protects the pangolin against bites and stings.

STATS

NO. 10 LEOPARD
Extreme Scores

Body Mass	4
Speed	6
Teeth and Claws	3
Killer Instinct	3
Prey	5

TOTAL SCORE 21/50

NO. 9 COYOTE
Extreme Scores

Body Mass	2
Speed	9
Teeth and Claws	6
Killer Instinct	4
Prey	2

TOTAL SCORE 23/50

NO. 8 POLAR BEAR
Extreme Scores

Body Mass	8
Speed	5
Teeth and Claws	4
Killer Instinct	2
Prey	5

TOTAL SCORE 24/50

NO. 7 ROYAL BENGAL TIGER
Extreme Scores

Body Mass	6
Speed	7
Teeth and Claws	4
Killer Instinct	5
Prey	3

TOTAL SCORE 25/50

NO. 6 CHEETAH
Extreme Scores

Body Mass	3
Speed	10
Teeth and Claws	2
Killer Instinct	4
Prey	7

TOTAL SCORE 26/50

NO. 5 GREAT HORNED OWL

Extreme Scores

Body Mass	1
Speed	9
Teeth and Claws	4
Killer Instinct	7
Prey	6

TOTAL SCORE: 27/50

NO. 4 NILE CROCODILE

Extreme Scores

Body Mass	7
Speed	3
Teeth and Claws	8
Killer Instinct	8
Prey	6

TOTAL SCORE: 32/50

NO. 3 AFRICAN LION

Extreme Scores

Body Mass	6
Speed	8
Teeth and Claws	5
Killer Instinct	7
Prey	8

TOTAL SCORE: 34/50

NO. 2 ORCA (KILLER WHALE)

Extreme Scores

Body Mass	10
Speed	5
Teeth and Claws	9
Killer Instinct	9
Prey	9

TOTAL SCORE: 42/50

NO. 1 GREAT WHITE SHARK

Extreme Scores

Body Mass	9
Speed	4
Teeth and Claws	10
Killer Instinct	10
Prey	10

TOTAL SCORE: 43/50

GLOSSARY

adapted (uh-DAP-tid) changed because of the environment; changed over time to be fit for the environment

ambush (AM-bush) to hide and then suddenly attack

arctic (ARK-tik) region around the North Pole

armor (AR-mur) a covering that protects the body

beak (BEEK) the hard, horn-shaped part of a bird's mouth

camouflage (KAM-uh-flahzh) the natural color or markings of an animal that helps it to blend in with its surroundings

climates (KLYE-mits) weather

cooperate (koh-OP-uh-rate) work together

efficient (uh-FISH-uhnt) able to work without wasting time or energy

environments (en-VYE-ruhn-muhnts) the plants, animals, and weather in a place

lunge (LUHNJ) to move forward quickly and without warning

mammals (MAM-uhlz) animals that are warm-blooded, nurse their young with milk, and have hair or fur on their skin

marine (muh-REEN) something that has to do with the sea

nostrils (NOSS-truhls) openings in the nose that are used for breathing and smelling

pale (PAYL) a color that is not bright, often whitish

perch (PURCH) a branch or bar on which a bird rests

predators (PRED-uh-turz) animals that hunt other animals for food

prey (PRAY) an animal that is hunted or caught for food

reptile (REP-tile) a cold-blooded animal that has dry, scaly skin, and uses lungs to breathe

talons (TAL-uhnz) claws of a predatory bird or other predatory animal

tropics (TROP-iks) the area near the equator that is hot all year

INDEX

A
Africa 6, 14, 18, 20, 27
African lion 20–21, 29
Alaska 8
arctic 10–11
Asia 6, 27

B
bald eagle 26
beak 16
big cats 6, 12–13, 14, 20–21

C
camouflage 5, 7, 11, 17
Canada 8
Central America 16
cheetah 14–15, 28
coyote 8–9, 28
crocodile 4, 18–19, 29

E
Europe 27
eyes 7, 8, 17, 18

F
feathers 17, 26
fish 10, 19, 23, 25, 26

G
grasslands 9, 14, 20
great horned owl 16–17, 29
great white shark 24–25, 29

I
India 12

J
jaws 10, 12, 18, 20, 24

L
leopard 6–7, 28

M
mammals 7, 9, 15, 21, 22, 27
Mexico 8

N
Nile crocodile 18–19, 29
North America 8, 16, 27
North Pole 10

O
orca (killer whale) 22–23, 29

P
Pakistan 12
pangolin 27
panthers 6
pods 22
polar bear 10–11, 28

R
reptile 18–19
Royal Bengal tiger 12–13, 28

S
smell 9, 24
South America 16, 27
spider 26

T
tail 18
talons 16, 26
tarantula 26

U
United States 26

V
vampire bat 27

W
wolverine 27